**Quality Coaches, Quality Sports:
National Standards for Sport Coaches,
Second Edition
2006**

Copyright © 2006

National Association for Sport and Physical Education, an association of the American Alliance for Health, Physical Education, Recreation and Dance.

All rights reserved.

Reproduction of this work in any form or by any electronic, mechanical, or other means, including photocopying or storage in any information retrieval system is expressly forbidden without the written permission of the publisher. Requests for permission to make copies of any part of the work should be mailed to: NASPE Publications, 1900 Association Drive, Reston, VA 20191-1599.

Address orders to: AAHPERD Publications, P.O. Box 385, Oxon Hill, MD 20750-0385, call 1-800-321-0789, or order online at www.aahperd.org/naspe.

Order Stock No. 304-10274

Printed in the United States of America.

ISBN: 0-88314-908-7

Suggested citation for this book:

> National Association for Sport and Physical Education. (2006). *Quality coaches, quality sports: National standards for sport coaches* (2nd ed.). Reston, VA: Author.

Second Edition Writing Committee

Jody Brylinsky, Committee Chair, Western Michigan University

Rick Albrecht, Grand Valley State University, MI

Dennis Docheff, Central Missouri State University

Tim Flannery, National Federation of State High School Associations, IN

Cathy Sellers, United States Olympic Committee, CO

Acknowledgements

1995 Sport Task Force (First Edition)

Vern Seefeldt, Task Force Chair, Youth Sport Institute, Michigan State University

Jack Acree, Boise City Schools, ID

Jody Brylinsky, Western Michigan University

David Feigley, Youth Sports Research Council, Rutgers University, NJ

Pat Sullivan, George Washington University, DC

Brent Steuerwald, Shenendehowa Central School District, NY

The National Association for Sport and Physical Education (NASPE) extends special thanks to those organizations that provided input through the revision process: United States Olympic Committee, National Federation of State High School Associations, as well as several of the national governing bodies of sport, many coaching education programs, and the NASPE sport councils: Coaches Council, National Council for Athletic Training, National Council of Secondary School Athletic Directors, and Youth Sport Coalition.

NASPE would like to acknowledge the quality coaching education programs that are being implemented across the country. Those currently accredited by the National Council for Accreditation of Coaching Education (NCACE) are:

American Youth Soccer Organization	Shippensburg University
Clarion University	Smith College
Georgia Southern University	Special Olympics International, Inc.
James Madison University	Virginia High School League
Kutztown University	

In addition, NASPE would like to recognize various quality coaching education programs already implemented across the country that contributed to ideas included in this document and have helped to shape the way for quality coaching education. These organizations include the Institute for the Study of Youth Sports' PACE program, the American Sport Education Program (ASEP), and various college and national governing body coaching education programs. Through the good work of organizations such as these, NASPE believes that coaching education will continue to evolve and gain the appropriate recognition and support it deserves.

NASPE would especially like to thank the Second Edition Writing Committee, chaired by Dr. Jody Brylinsky, for volunteering their time and expertise to the revision of the standards document and for setting the bar high for quality coaching education.

Table of Contents

Supporting Organizations for National Standards for Sport Coaches 1

Introduction 3

National Standards for Sport Coaches—Domains, Standards, and Benchmarks 7

The Three Levels of Coaching Education 25

Topical Reference 29

Resources for Coaching Education Programs 33

Glossary 39

NASPE Resources 41

Supporting Organizations for National Standards for Sport Coaches

Science/Medical
American College of Sports Medicine (ACSM)
Association for the Advancement of Applied Sport Psychology (AAASP)
The Center for Sports Parenting
Coalition to Prevent Sports Eye Injuries
The Cooper Institute
Institute for the Study of Youth Sports (ISYS)
National Athletic Trainers' Association (NATA)
National Center for Sports Safety
The Sports Medicine Center at Akron Children's Hospital

Physically Challenged
The American Association of Adapted Sports Programs
Special Olympics North America
United States Association of Blind Athletes

School Sports
Greenville County School District
National Association of Collegiate Directors of Athletics (NACDA)
National Association of Intercollegiate Athletics (NAIA)
National Federation of State High School Associations (NFHS)
Northeast Ohio Interscholastic Athletic Administrators Association
Oxnard Union High School District
Virginia High School League

Sport Organizations
American Athletic Union (AAU)
American Sport Education Program (ASEP)
American Volleyball Coaches Association
American Youth Soccer Organization (AYSO)
Catholic Youth Organization (CYO)
Cavar Sports Academy
Center for Physical Activity and Sport, Boise State University
The Center for the Advancement of Responsible Youth Sports at California State University, Fullerton
Dave Barrett's Kids in Action
D.C. Coaches Association
Institute for Sport Coaching
Jewish Community Center Association
Mighigan High School Coaching Association
National Council of Youth Sports (NCYS)
National Football Foundation Center for Youth Development through Sport at Springfield College
National Strength and Conditioning Association (NSCA)
New York Road Runners Foundation
North American Youth Sport Institute
PONY Baseball and Softball
Pop Warner Little Scholars
Sporting Goods Manufacturers Association (SGMA)
Rutgers Youth Sports Research Council
US Youth Soccer
WinStar Foundation
Women's Sports Foundation

National Governing Bodies
United States Olympic Committee (USOC)
United States Orienteering Federation (USOF)
United States Tennis Association (USTA)
USA Badminton
USA Diving
USA Football
USA National KarateDo Federation
US Ski and Snowboard Association (USSA)
USA Table Tennis
USA Team Handball
USA Volleyball
USA Water Polo
USA Wrestling

Colleges and Universities
Athens State University
Ball State University
Boise State University
Brigham Young University
Butler University
California State University, Chico-Department of Kinesiology
Clarion University
Clemson University
Coastal Carolina University
College of St. Benedict/St. John's University
Eastern Michigan University
Georgia Southern University
Grand Valley State University
Huntingdon College
Husson College
James Madison University
Kutztown University
The Laboratory for the Study of Intercollegiate Athletics (LSIA)
Lee University
Middle Tennessee State University
North Carolina State University
Norwich University Physical Education Department
Ohio University
Presbyterian College
Rhode Island College
St. Edwards University Kinesiology Department
St. John's University
Shippensburg University
State University of New York (SUNY), College at Brockport
State University of New York (SUNY), Cortland
Sullivan County Community College
Tri-State University
United States Sports Academy
University of Akron
University of Southern Mississippi
Weber State University
West Virginia University
Western Michigan University
Winona State University
Xavier University

Recreation
City of El Paso
City of Gary Department of Public Parks
Gang Alternatives Program
Indianapolis Parks and Recreation
Kansas Association for Health, Physical Education, Recreation and Dance (KAHPERD)
Massachusetts Association for Health, Physical Education, Recreation and Dance (MAHPERD)
Midwest District of the American Alliance for Health, Physical Education, Recreation and Dance
Minnesota Association for Health, Physical Education, Recreation and Dance (MAHPERD)
National Recreation and Park Associations (NRPA)
National Rifle Association Shooting Coach Education Program
South Carolina Association for Physical Education and Sport (SCAHPERD)
Tennessee Association for Health, Physical Education, Recreation and Dance (TAHPERD)
Texas Association for Health, Physical Education, Recreation and Dance (TAHPERD)

AAHPERD Associations
American Association for Physical Activity and Recreation (AAPAR) of the American Alliance for Health, Physical Education, Recreation and Dance (AAHPERD)
National Association for Girls and Women in Sport (NAGWS) of the American Alliance for Health, Physical Education, Recreation and Dance (AAHPERD)

Introduction

Many people have suggested that coaching is as much an art as it is a science. And while we should not attempt to reduce the practice of coaching to a "technoscience," we can and should be clear on what effective coaches should know, value, and be able to do. The National Association for Sport and Physical Education (NASPE) published the *National Standards for Athletic Coaches* (NSAC) in 1995. Over 100 sport organizations agreed that a core body of knowledge existed from which to develop coaching expertise. The 37 standards grouped into eight domains identified the scientific and practical competencies that administrators, athletes, and the public should expect of sport coaches at various levels of experience.

Role and Purpose of Standards

The *National Standards for Sport Coaches* (2006) provide direction for coaching educators, sport administrators, coaches, athletes and their families, and the public regarding the skills and knowledge that coaches should possess. They reflect the fundamental actions and orientations that administrators, athletes, and the public should expect of sport coaches at various levels of competition. The expansion of knowledge applicable to coaching enables us to continually improve standards related to the care, health, performance, and safety of athletes. Because coaches are teachers and mentors who influence and spend considerable time with athletes, they must have resources to improve their knowledge and skills and meet changing expectations on and off the field. It is imperative that coaches aspire to and achieve high standards as well as have resources available to assist them in gaining necessary skills and knowledge.

These standards should encourage individuals, including those at the volunteer level, to gain the qualifications necessary to coach athletes with diverse skills and potential. Coaching education program directors should use these standards to evaluate the impact of coaches on the sport experiences of athletes. Adopting the standards and assisting coaches in meeting them improves opportunities for coaches and athletes to successfully excel in sports and skill development. Coaching education programs should use these standards to construct curriculum for training previously underrepresented populations in the coaching industry, including minorities, women, and prospective coaches with a disability.

These standards provide a guide for meeting expectations set by the Americans with Disabilities Act. An increased commitment to include athletes and coaches with disabilities is embedded in these standards. While the needs of athletes with disabilities are sometimes met most effectively by coaches, administrators, and trainers who posses specialized competencies, these standards will assist coaches as they maximize participation among all athletes in a supportive, reassuring, and safe environment. The standards also assume that individuals with disabilities can and should be effective coaches.

The domains, standards, and benchmarks outlined in this guide are based on the most recent scientific information related to coaching. New information, laws, and technologies will require that this document be reviewed and updated regularly. The goal is to provide knowledge that maximizes the enjoyment, safety, and positive skill development of athletes.

Explanation of the Standards Revision Process

The initial NSAC outlined the knowledge, skills, and values associated with coaching sport, and as with all NASPE publications, an ongoing review and timely revision was expected. To represent the most current trends in the coaching world, NASPE reviews and updates publications every five to seven years. This ensures that particular audiences receive current information on a regular cycle. In the changing world of sport, coaches need a quality education system to stay prepared to work effectively with athletes. These standards serve this need.

NASPE called on experts from national governing bodies of sport, the United States Olympic Committee, National Federation of State High School Associations, and NASPE leadership to review and revise the 1995 version of the standards. The 1995 standards were accepted by over 100 organizations, and therefore the intent of these revisions was to update them and make them more user-friendly, rather than completely revamping them. After reviewing prominent coaching education literature and soliciting feedback from coaching educators and policy-makers, the original domains were revised to be more consistent with current best practices and sport resources. The second edition is more straightforward than the 1995 version, but no skill components were discarded from the original version; instead they were incorporated into specific domains to increase clarity and eliminate redundancies.

The revised *National Standards for Sport Coaches* (NSSC) is organized into eight domains that more accurately describe significant coaching responsibilities. Each of the 40 standards are presented with an explanation of its purpose. Each standard is accompanied by benchmarks that provide concrete examples of actions and orientations that constitute coaching competence. The original NSAC identified over 350 competencies reflecting varying degrees of proficiency in applying a specified skill. The revised benchmarks are not intended to be an exhaustive list of potential performance indicators, but rather performance guides to be used in developing and assessing coaching competence. By design, the NSSC provide a framework that can be applied and used to identify coaching competencies within the structure and context of any sport or coaching program.

Summary of Major Changes

The second edition standards are applicable across all sports and at all competitive levels. This document provides a clear outline of what coaches should know and be able to do. If a sport or coaching program covers the information contained in this book, the programs can be expected to prepare qualified coaches.

The major difference between the first and second edition is that there are fewer competencies listed under each standard in the second edition. The second edition does not try to list all competencies, but it is understood that quality coaching education provides coverage and exposure to appropriate areas that are outlined in the benchmarks under each standard. The benchmarks highlight important areas under each standard that should be expanded on depending on what level of coach is being trained and in what social context the standard is being applied (e.g., a volunteer coach should know how to recognize an emergency and take action to care for the athletes involved, but may not necessarily need to provide care in the way of extensive treatment and rehabilitation).

Another difference between the first and second editions is the format of the domains, standards, and benchmarks. In this edition, a narrative accompanies each standard to provide a detailed explanation of the standard. This provides perspective for the coach educators and frames the benchmarks in appropriate areas.

The benchmarks are not grouped into levels; instead, all coaches should have some awareness or application of each of the standards. Sport and coaching organizations may develop levels of application in a manner suitable to specific programs of coaching development. These levels are outlined in more detail on pages 25 through 28.

The standards and subsequent benchmarks represent a body of knowledge that can be applied to every level of coach responsibility. For coaches with limited responsibilities (i.e., short competitive seasons, beginning level skills and tactics, emphasis on participation versus competition), each standard reflects basic benchmarks for behavior. Where coaches have greater levels of responsibility (i.e., longer sequential seasons, advanced skills and tactics, competition pressures) more specified performance indicators would be warranted. Coaches should consider the requirement of additional, specialized qualifications depending on the needs of the athletes involved, including sport-specific and/or level-specific information. Thus, the emphasis of this document is on the basic knowledge required of coaches at each level of professional development as they progress from a novice to a highly skilled professional, master coach.

The eight domains identified in this document are used to categorize the standards that reflect the scope of coaching responsibilities.

Domain 1: Philosophy and Ethics is a new domain title that reflects the reorganization and prioritization of standards previously found in the domain *Social and Psychological Aspects of Coaching*. Standards 1 through 4 more clearly articulate the importance of an athlete-centered coaching philosophy and professional accountability for fair play by all.

Domain 2: Safety and Injury Prevention maintains the core standards of coach responsibility for providing safe conditions and appropriate actions when emergencies arise. It also addresses the need for coaches to know how to effectively participate as part of the sports medicine team. Administrative duties concerning injury prevention, such as physical exams and report documents are now reorganized into *Domain 7: Organization and Administration*. Standards 5 through 11 establish expectations for coaches to create and maintain a safe and healthy sport experience for all athletes.

Domain 3: Physical Conditioning is an updated and more behavioral description of coaching responsibilities in the areas of physiological training, nutrition education, and maintaining a drug-free environment. Standards 12 through 15 highlight the importance of using scientific principles in designing and implementing conditioning programs for natural performance gains. Specific attention is given to body composition and weight management issues as well as awareness of contraindicated activities and overtraining concerns. The important role physical conditioning plays in preventing and recovering from injuries is also included.

Domain 4: Growth and Development maintains its original title and importance in the scope of coaching responsibilities. Standards 16 through 18 and related benchmarks more clearly identify developmental considerations in designing practice and competition to enhance the physical, social, and emotional growth of athletes. New to this area is the identification of the coach's role in creating an inclusive learning environment that leads all athletes to feel welcome and supported and to have experiences that foster leadership skills.

Domain 5: Teaching and Communication takes on a new look of identifying standards for sound instructional strategies and interpersonal behavior of the coach. Responsibilities for creating a positive coaching style while maximizing learning and enjoyment are established in Standards 19 through 26. Greater emphasis is placed on individualizing instruction, empowering communication skills, and using good management techniques in designing practices. While effective instruction should enhance athlete motivation, additional attention is drawn to the critical influence coaching behavior plays in developing self-determined and satisfied athletes. Also new are benchmarks that make coaches aware of their role in mitigating bullying and harassment in the sport environment.

Domain 6: Sport Skills and Tactics is more focused on the need for coaches to have basic sport knowledge and be able to apply it to the competitive environment. Standards 27 through 29 focus on using basic sport skills and acceptance of prescribed rules in developing team and individual competitive tactics. New emphasis is placed on planning that is age-appropriate, sequential, and progressive. New benchmarks highlight the coach's role in making tactical and personnel decisions during competition. Also new are more definitive expectations for scouting and game analysis.

Domain 7: Organization and Administration has been streamlined to better identify how the coach provides resources in the daily operation and management of the sport program. Standards 30 through 36 include risk management responsibilities as well as effective use of human and financial resources. Again, coaches play an important role in sharing administrative duties with any number of other stakeholders in maximizing the sport experience.

Domain 8: Evaluation is a new domain that captures the numerous assessment skills necessary to be an effective coach. Standards 37 through 40 identify the ongoing evaluation responsibilities of the coach in areas such as personnel selection, on-time reflection of practice effectiveness, progress toward individual athlete goals, game management, and program evaluation. Creating a meaningful evaluation process for self-reflection and professional growth is also now included in this area.

Summary

Through the revision process, NASPE had two main goals in mind:
1. Clearly articulate a conceptual framework that establishes coaching as a profession.
2. Provide a user-friendly document with which all coaching organizations can implement a comprehensive, quality training program.

Due to the acceptance of the first edition's (1995) standards by programs across the country, NASPE anticipates wide acceptance of the second edition. Throughout its years of involvement in the coaching arena, NASPE has witnessed adoption of its standards at all levels of coaching education, from established youth sport programs to colleges and universities. Programs that have been in existence for years have evaluated their current programs to determine how well they are addressing the national standards.

The optimal sport experience can only be brought about by caring and professionally trained coaches. Parents across the country send their children to practices and events with the expectation that adult supervision will bring about positive sport outcomes and maximal learning and development. Youths and young adults are willing to invest a great deal of time, money, and personal identity in developing their chosen sport skills. A systematic discourse of what coaches should know and do will advance all of our efforts in producing competent, qualified coaches.

Domains, Standards, & Benchmarks

Domain 1 — Philosophy and Ethics

It is imperative that the coach establishes a coaching philosophy that focuses on the safety, development, and well-being of the athlete. As a key leadership figure, the coach must model and teach appropriate behavior in all aspects of coaching and maintain ethical conduct during practices and competitions.

The coach will:

Standard 1: Develop and implement an athlete-centered coaching philosophy.

A well-developed coaching philosophy provides expectations for behaviors that reflect priorities and values of the coach. An appropriate coaching perspective focuses on maximizing the positive benefits of sport participation for each athlete.

Benchmarks
- Identify and communicate reasons for entering the coaching profession.
- Develop an athlete-centered coaching philosophy that aligns with the organizational mission and goals.
- Communicate the athlete-centered coaching philosophy in verbal and written form to athletes, parents/guardians, and program staff.
- Welcome all eligible athletes and implement strategies that encourage the participation of disadvantaged and disabled athletes.
- Manage athlete behavior consistent with an athlete-centered coaching philosophy.

Standard 2: Identify, model, and teach positive values learned through sport participation.

The coach plays a key role in teaching and demonstrating the positive values gained through the sport experience. The coach must structure opportunities for development of values that can be applied inside and outside of sport.

Benchmarks
- Provide opportunities for input from the community regarding positive values taught in the sport program.
- Practice respect for diverse populations.

- Facilitate and reinforce the development of positive character traits through team policies and procedures.
- Teach that winning is a worthwhile goal of positive sport participation and losing is an opportunity to grow and improve.
- Teach the value of lifetime fitness and wellness throughout the training process.
- Engage athletes in dialogue and problem solving to promote positive character development when ethical issues arise.
- Plan and implement coaching techniques that emphasize the importance of enjoying sport participation.

Standard 3: Teach and reinforce responsible personal, social, and ethical behavior of all people involved in the sport program.

The coach has a responsibility to facilitate development of positive behaviors in and through sport. Sport settings require personal and social responsibility in participants as well as provide opportunities for teaching these characteristics.

Benchmarks
- Apply the rules of the sport in an ethical manner.
- Demonstrate and teach respect for officials, parents, guardians, athletes, and opponents.
- Reinforce positive social behaviors in athletes by respecting effort and stressing personal improvement and self-control.
- Be proactive in preventing bullying and/or hazing behavior on the part of athletes, staff, or spectators and stop the acts immediately. Teach athletes how to effectively react to bullying/hazing and how to safely become an ally for victims.

Standard 4: Demonstrate ethical conduct in all facets of the sport program.

The coach is an influential role model, as their actions are strong indicators of their beliefs. In order to ensure ethical conduct in sport, coaches must reflect on, monitor, and adjust their behavior for consistency with an ethical, athlete-centered approach to coaching.

Benchmarks
- Model good sporting behavior by adhering to both the spirit and the letter of the rules.
- Exhibit self-control and self-discipline, recognizing the effect coaching behavior may have on athletes, officials, and spectators.
- Use positive language and actions that create a safe, non-threatening, and respectful environment for all athletes to learn and compete.
- Develop and maintain a professional relationship with athletes and other coaches that clearly separates the role of the coach from that of parent, friend, or counselor.
- Ensure that qualified individuals are present to officiate all competition.
- Use personal and official power in a responsible manner to reduce the potential for sexual harassment and athlete abuse.
- Discuss the negative influence of gambling on sport.

Domain 2—Safety and Injury Prevention

The coach is often the first and only responder in the event of an accident or injury and should be properly trained in injury prevention and first responder emergency care. The coach must recognize high-risk situations, as well as unsafe equipment, facilities, and environmental conditions in order to ensure the safety of the athletes and make necessary modifications to the playing environment should unsafe conditions exist.

The coach will:

Standard 5: Prevent injuries by providing safe facilities.

Sport and sport settings have inherent risks that require coaches to maximize safety for all participants. The coach must be familiar with all standards and guidelines regarding facility safety, inspection, and maintenance. The coach must continuously work to monitor and maintain full compliance with established standards and guidelines.

Benchmarks
- Assure that facilities and structures are installed, secured, and protected according to safety specifications.
- Regularly inspect and monitor sport facilities to detect and reduce the risk of environmental, structural, or surface hazards on a regular basis.
- Modify plans for practice and competition after assessing potentially unsafe conditions that may exist.

Standard 6: Ensure that all necessary protective equipment is available, properly fitted, and used appropriately.

The proper selection, use, and maintenance of equipment are critical to minimizing risk to athletes. Equipment must be checked on a regular basis. The coach must provide athletes with clear instruction on the care and use of protective equipment.

Benchmarks
- Ensure that athletes are provided with equipment that meets recognized safety standards as required by appropriate governing agencies.
- Monitor fitting and maintenance of all equipment for athletes.
- Ensure that all athletes know how to properly select, use, and care for protective equipment.

Standard 7: Monitor environmental conditions and modify participation as needed to ensure the health and safety of participants.

It is the coach's responsibility to protect athletes from adverse effects of climate-related factors. Effective planning for safety includes the consideration of environmental factors such as temperature, humidity, altitude, air quality, lightning, and other factors that may affect athlete health, performance, and safety.

Benchmarks
- Provide information to assistant coaches, athletes, and parents/guardians on environmental safety in sport.
- Facilitate appropriate hydration based on relevant environmental factors for all athletes.
- Stop or modify play in accordance with rules or policies designed to protect athletes from environmental dangers.

Standard 8: Identify physical conditions that predispose athletes to injuries.

Athletes often join teams with pre-existing conditions or previous injuries that would preclude them from certain exercises or drills. The coach should be aware of such injuries and modify drills and exercises as appropriate.

Benchmarks
- Ensure that clearance for athletes to participate fully or partially in practices or contests is given by a parent, guardian, and/or medical professional.
- Recognize health status, body structure, and physical conditions that predispose athletes to common injuries specific to the sport.
- Be aware that an athlete's lack of sleep and/or emotional state could warrant a change in practice plans.

Standard 9: Recognize injuries and provide immediate and appropriate care.

The coach must be able to implement an established emergency action plan. The coach should be able to assess the severity of an injury, provide first responder emergency care (should there be no trained medical professional available), and contact emergency medical personnel when needed.

Benchmarks
- Have athlete medical information readily available.
- Implement an appropriate action plan for emergency first aid and CPR in all venues.
- Provide and be able to use an appropriately stocked first aid kit.
- Encourage athletes to openly communicate concerns about pain and discomfort; dispel any "play through pain" attitudes.
- Apply standard procedures designed to minimize exposure to blood-borne pathogens.
- Know when professional medical care is required for an injured athlete and how to most efficiently access such care.
- Allow athletes the time to recover fully from injury before returning to play.

Standard 10: Facilitate a coordinated sports health care program that includes prevention, care, and management of injuries.

While the coach should be certified in First Aid and CPR in order to be able to provide first responder care, the coach should also use the resources available to them in order to provide a safe playing environment for the athletes. Resources can include medical professionals certified to handle prevention, care, and management of injuries.

Benchmarks
- Establish regular communication with parents/guardians that facilitates prevention, reporting, and care of injuries.
- Consult with a certified athletic trainer or physician for assistance in understanding the physical needs of athletes.
- Clarify chain of command in allowing athletes to return to play once an athlete is referred to a medical provider for care of an injury.
- Modify coaching techniques when warranted by medical, physical, and emotional needs.

Standard 11: Identify and address the psychological implications of injury.

Knowledge of psychological factors that are associated with injury is critical in helping athletes avoid or recover from injury. The coach should know the typical reactions to injury and when various psychological techniques can be used to help make positive adjustments in the recovery process. Reducing fear of re-injury, lowering anxiety over loss of playing time, and maintaining normal social interactions with teammates assist in the recovery process.

Benchmarks
- Recognize psychological conditions that predispose athletes to injury and make adjustments in training and conditioning regimes.
- Provide a supportive environment that helps the injured athlete maintain social interactions with teammates and coaching staff.
- Use appropriate mental training techniques to reduce anxiety and fear of re-injury and possible adjustment of performance expectations after returning to play.
- Be proactive in building athlete self-confidence and self-esteem during the rehabilitation process.
- Use appropriate motivational techniques to assist injured athletes in maintaining adherence to rehabilitation protocol.
- Refer athletes to appropriate professional services when the signs of poor psychological adjustment to injury exist.

Domain 3—Physical Conditioning

Sport requires proper physical preparation in order to perform safely and effectively. The coach is responsible for implementing research-based, developmentally appropriate drills and teaching techniques that support athlete development while maintaining safety. The coach should encourage healthful decisions by the athlete to promote healthy lifestyles and low-risk training practices.

The coach will:

Standard 12: Design programs of training, conditioning, and recovery that properly utilize exercise physiology and biomechanical principles.

Use of appropriate conditioning practices increases opportunities for successful sport performance and helps prevent injuries. Knowledge of exercise physiology and biomechanics is critical in the design of effective conditioning programs. In addition, coaches must consider the proper use of rest and recovery in specific training programs. Design of programs includes consideration of individual athlete characteristics and specific sport characteristics and demands.

Benchmarks
- Present conditioning as a prerequisite for athletes to perform at their best, not as punishment.
- Know the components of physical fitness and prescribe appropriate levels of each in relation to age- and sport-specific demands.
- Consider the influence of body composition in planning for appropriate practice and conditioning.
- Create sport-specific warm-up and cool-down activities that accomplish physical and psychological readiness prior to instruction.
- Plan a variety of conditioning programs that demonstrate knowledge of physiological responses to physical activity and athletic performance through all phases of the sport season.
- Utilize sound biomechanical principles in the development of training programs that maximize the structural advantages of each athlete.

- Monitor athletes to allow for adequate recovery time to avoid overtraining and maximize windows of optimal training.
- Identify and use time efficient cross-training conditioning activities that maximize development of more than one system at a time.
- Avoid training/conditioning activities that are potentially harmful or contraindicated for athletes.

Standard 13: Teach and encourage proper nutrition for optimal physical and mental performance and overall good health.

The coach must understand and teach appropriate nutrition and weight management practices. Counseling athletes about healthy eating is an important part of preparing athletes for sport performance. Proper nutrition and hydration are necessary to fuel the body.

Benchmarks
- Assist athletes in timing and selection of food options to fuel optimal energy production for practices and contests.
- Assist athletes in regulating safe levels of hydration.
- Provide accurate and timely information to athletes and parents/guardians about sound nutritional principles as part of training and preparation for competition.
- Provide accurate and timely information about body composition and healthy weight management.
- Be proactive in identifying potential eating disorders and referring athletes for appropriate professional assistance.

Standard 14: Be an advocate for drug-free sport participation and provide accurate information about drugs and supplements.

Many drugs and supplements are available to athletes with little information about the long-term impact on health. The coach has a great influence over lifestyle practices of their athletes and must ensure that players have accurate and adequate information about the effects of drug and supplement use and abuse. The coach must not encourage the use of drugs and/or supplements as a means of enhancing athletic performance.

Benchmarks
- Obtain current, research-based information related to supplements and their potential impact on performance and health.
- Provide parents/guardians, athletes, and staff with information on the effects of drugs, supplements, and prescribed medications on athletic performance, weight, and health.
- Intervene and/or refer athletes to appropriate experts when significant changes in body composition, physical appearance, and personality that may be drug-related are observed.
- Make clear to all athletes the established, negative consequences of using a banned substance, alcohol, tobacco, and other drugs as they relate to team rules, program policies, the law, and overall health.
- Identify and acknowledge the social, emotional, and psychological pressures that make athletes susceptible to drug/supplement use and teach alternate strategies to mediate these factors.

Standard 15: Plan conditioning programs to help athletes return to full participation following injury.

Proper conditioning is critical following an athletic injury. The coach must ensure that the health and well-being of the participant is the first priority when making decisions about returning to participation. Following the direction of qualified medical personnel regarding athletes' reconditioning programs is the only way to ensure safety and success in returning the athlete to full participation.

Benchmarks
- Require written permission from a qualified medical professional prior to allowing an injured athlete to engage in physical conditioning.
- Maintain regular communication with the physicians and parents/guardians of injured athletes about relevant demands of the sport in preparing conditioning programs following injury.
- Ensure that athletes follow direction of medical personnel in the rehabilitation of an injury and are allowed sufficient time to fully recover before returning to play.

Domain 4—Growth and Development

The coach should be knowledgeable about the age and skill levels of their athletes. By recognizing the patterns of cognitive, motor, emotional, and social development, the coach can create effective learning environments that allow athletes to progress and improve at different rates. The coach should be properly trained to recognize the need to modify practice and competitive strategies to accommodate the athlete's readiness for competition.

The coach will:

Standard 16: Apply knowledge of how developmental change influences the learning and performance of sport skills.

Athletes change physically, psychologically, and emotionally as they mature; therefore, appropriate instruction and training strategies may be different for each developmental stage. The coach must recognize changing developmental patterns in athletes and modify instruction to support individual athlete's specific needs and developmental characteristics.

Benchmarks
- Identify sequence of movements and critical environmental demands of a motor task to determine athlete readiness to learn the skill.
- Develop instruction and practice opportunities that enhance the learning of motor skills based on developmental readiness of the athlete.
- Analyze motor performance in relation to development of individual body structures and systems.
- Recognize that athletes may be early or late maturers, which may not be related to future success.
- Support athletes encountering developmental problems such as eye-hand coordination, visual training needs, growth spurts, and/or maturational problems with additional instruction or referral.

Standard 17: Facilitate the social and emotional growth of athletes by supporting a positive sport experience and lifelong participation in physical activity.

Participation in sport can promote healthy growth in all dimensions of physical and mental health. The coach makes a positive impact in the social and emotional development of athletes by recognizing that sport is important in providing lifelong support for a healthy lifestyle.

Benchmarks
- Acknowledge the social-emotional issues that may affect athletes of different ages.
- Help athletes develop motivational and cognitive readiness by providing positive verbal and nonverbal performance feedback and clarifying causes of success and failure.
- Support a balanced lifestyle, allowing time for athletes to participate in a variety of activities outside of sport.
- Emphasize lifelong enjoyment of physical activity as a goal of sport participation.
- Assist athletes in coping with the complexity of managing sport participation and life stressors.
- Provide activities that help athletes recognize their physical and emotional limits.
- Evaluate athlete training and progress in light of risks for overtraining or over-use injuries.

Standard 18: Provide athletes with responsibility and leadership opportunities as they mature.

Sport provides an atmosphere for trial and error through practice and competition. Sport also allows opportunity for athletes to be challenged by additional responsibility. Through these opportunities, athletes learn how to deal with conflict, engage in problem solving, and seek positive resolutions. The coach should engage athletes in opportunities that nurture leadership and teamwork that can be learned on the field and exhibited in life.

Benchmarks
- Teach and encourage athletes to take responsibility for their actions in adhering to team rules.
- Design practices to allow for athlete input and self-evaluation.
- Communicate to athletes their responsibility in maintaining physical and mental readiness for athletic participation and preparation for competition.
- Encourage athletes to practice leadership skills and engage in problem solving.
- Provide athletes with different tools to manage conflict.
- Provide specific opportunities for athletes to mentor others.

Domain 5—Teaching and Communication

The coach must plan and implement organized practices so that athletes have a positive learning experience. In addition to understanding the fundamentals of the sport, the coach should use a variety of systematic instructional techniques to provide a positive learning environment and maximize the potential of each athlete. Furthermore, the coach needs to be aware of his or her own expectations of an athlete's potential and how it impacts athlete performance.

The coach will:

Standard 19: **Provide a positive learning environment that is appropriate to the characteristics of the athletes and goals of the program.**

Practice plans and contest strategies should be appropriate for the age, skill level, and experience of the athletes. The coach needs to consider these factors in the design of drills, grouping of athletes, position assignments, and contest management. The coach must design and maintain a positive learning environment.

Benchmarks
- Treat each athlete as an individual.
- Implement activities that foster team cohesion.
- Show acceptance of athletes of all abilities by reacting positively when mistakes are made.
- Offer corrective instruction and give encouragement consistent with expectations for athlete success.
- Implement behavioral management and positive discipline strategies that are appropriate for the athletes.
- Promote opportunity within sport by encouraging appropriate and equal participation regardless of race, ethnicity, gender, and socio-economic status.

Standard 20: **Develop and monitor goals for the athletes and program.**

The coach outlines the goals for the season in collaboration with athletes and staff. Through a goal-setting process, athletes can define success and assess progress in skill development, tactical lessons, and teamwork. The coach may also assess the performances of the sport program staff and readjust team goals as necessary.

Benchmarks
- Set goals for each practice and competition.
- Facilitate the goal-setting process by providing opportunities for athletes and program staff to participate in setting realistic, performance-based goals.
- Utilize pre- and post-assessment of skills to determine and adjust appropriate individual goals.
- Review and modify goals with athletes and staff throughout the season to be sure goals remain realistic and challenging.
- Facilitate a mastery goal orientation for each athlete, focusing on effort and self-determination.

Standard 21: **Organize practice based on a seasonal or annual practice plan to maintain motivation, manage fatigue, and allow for peak performance at the appropriate time.**

Practice plans should be based on the skills required for the sport, the athletes' current level of skill attainment, and what must be taught to improve performance. The coach recognizes optimal times for physical and tactical improvements and designs practice plans using appropriate periodization principles.

Benchmarks
- Identify and establish season and practice objectives to meet desired outcomes in skill development, knowledge of sport, physical conditioning, and personal social development.
- Construct monthly, weekly, and daily practice plans based on seasonal goals.
- Prepare practice plans that reflect reasonable time allowances for skill development.
- Share plans with staff members and athletes.

Standard 22: Plan and implement daily practice activities that maximize time on task and available resources.

Creating an orderly environment is essential in implementing safe and effective practices. Planning what resources are necessary and how to best utilize space and time increases athlete motivation and learning outcomes. The coach communicates to athletes what is planned for the practice and is expected of their participation.

Benchmarks
- Secure sufficient staffing to maximize athlete supervision and instruction.
- Organize equipment and space to allow for easy regrouping of athletes and transition to next activity.
- Reduce wait time by adequately preparing drills and having sufficient equipment ready for use.
- Provide staff and athletes with a clear indication of what is planned for the practice, the objectives, and possible sequence of activities.
- Provide athletes with written descriptions and diagrams of new drills or team tactics prior to instruction.
- Group athletes according to learning objectives and consideration of safety, motivation, and team morale.

Standard 23: Utilize appropriate instructional strategies to facilitate athlete development and performance.

The coach must use a variety of instructional strategies to meet the needs of all athletes. The coach also provides specific progressions for learning and practicing skills from simple motor patterns to more difficult, complex skills. Practice and competitive experiences should facilitate learning new skills, refining existing skills, and reteaching of skills that need improvement and applications to competition.

Benchmarks
- Design teaching progressions for developing sport-specific skills based on best practices in teaching and learning principles
- Design instructional processes that include verbal, visual, and tactical cues that address different learning styles.
- Utilize a variety of instructional methods encouraging learning through problem-solving activities and games-based learning.
- Plan the order of practice activities to provide sufficient practice time for skill acquisition and retention.
- Utilize peer/athlete demonstration to heighten athlete confidence and sense of control in the learning process.
- Use appropriate technology to analyze performance in both practice and competition.
- Consider motivational issues associated with correcting errors and selecting techniques for re-teaching.

Standard 24: Teach and incorporate mental skills to enhance performance and reduce sport anxiety.

Mental skill training assists the athlete in improving athletic performance. The variety of tools available allow the athlete to manage stress and direct their focus on their performance.

Benchmarks
- Demonstrate appropriate use of intrinsic and extrinsic rewards to enhance motivation and learning.
- Share with athletes effective stress management coping strategies.
- Utilize sound mental skills to build athlete self-confidence.
- Help athletes to develop a mental game plan that includes pregame preparation, a contingency plan for errors during competition, and how to avoid competitive stress.
- Help athletes improve concentration by learning attention control strategies.

Standard 25: Use effective communication skills to enhance individual learning, group success, and enjoyment in the sport experience.

Effective communication, both sending and receiving information, is necessary for the athlete to learn. Communication from the coach should be clear, positive, and meaningful during instruction as well as during competition. In order to provide the athlete with the best opportunity to succeed, the coach must also become an effective listener.

Benchmarks
- Use terminology of the specific sport necessary to communicate intended outcomes and activities with athletes and coaches.
- Communicate high achievement expectations to athletes by providing positive feedback and instructive comments relative to athlete performance.
- Establish an orderly environment to gain the athlete's attention prior to giving instruction. Check for athlete understanding and comprehension before moving on.
- Provide feedback on individual and team performance, linking individual contribution to overall team goals.
- Use professional and age-appropriate language at all times. Use nonsexist and inclusive language.
- Pace instructional cues to allow athletes time to process information and respond with questions.
- Avoid overcommunicating both in practice and in game situations.

Standard 26: Demonstrate and utilize appropriate and effective motivational techniques to enhance athlete performance and satisfaction.

Motivating athletes to focus on learning, improving their skills, and performing at an optimal level is a major responsibility for coaches. The coach understands principles of motivation and develops and maintains a repertoire of positive strategies for helping athletes maximize their success and enjoyment of sport.

Benchmarks
- Identify and implement positive motivational strategies.
- Recognize individual athletes' unique motivational needs and challenges.
- Prevent burnout by designing interventions that are based on understanding of motivation and overtraining principles.
- Create a learning environment that focuses on both effort and achievement.
- Provide accurate and supportive feedback on the causes of success or failure.
- Never use physical activity or peer pressure as a means of disciplining athlete behavior.
- Build confidence in the team and individual by reinforcing past success and other sources of self-efficacy.

Domain 6—Sport Skills and Tactics

The art and science of coaching includes developing skills of all team members into an efficient and successful group. Knowing how to utilize athletes' abilities to maximize meaningful participation and team success relies on up-to-date understanding of specific sport skills and game tactics.

The coach will:

Standard 27: Know the skills, elements of skill combinations, and techniques associated with the sport being coached.

The coach should have knowledge commensurate with the level of sport and athlete being coached. Activities should be designed to be age- and skill-appropriate. Skills and tactics should be focused on the goals and objectives of the program and athlete.

Benchmarks
- Identify and facilitate accurate demonstration of cognitive, affective, and physical skills essential to the specific sport.
- Identify and provide feedback on performance of basic techniques.
- Incorporate individual tactics that are safe and consistent with sport rules and stated program goals.
- Analyze and adjust skills and tactics based on success and areas needing improvement throughout the season.

Standard 28: Identify, develop, and apply competitive sport strategies and specific tactics appropriate for the age and skill levels of the participating athletes.

The coach must maintain up-to-date and innovative coaching techniques by attending workshops and clinics from accredited providers in order to provide appropriate direction to their athletes. The coach must be able to provide instruction on skills and tactics in the practice setting in order to better translate skills into game situations. Strategies should be implemented based on previously learned techniques appropriate to the age and ability level of the athletes.

Benchmarks
- Incorporate competitive strategies and team tactics that are consistent with sport rules and coaching philosophy.
- Design situation-specific tactics that compliment the abilities of the athletes and unique characteristics of the competitive situation.
- Involve athletes in selecting competitive strategies and facilitate effective strategic decision making by athletes.
- Assign positions and develop line-ups, orders, and rotations that reflect the capabilities and readiness of the athletes
- Make decisions that will allow for adjustments during competition.

Standard 29: Use scouting methods for planning practices, game preparation, and game analysis.

Preparing the athlete and/or team appropriately for competition is the responsibility of the coach. The coach should use appropriate scouting techniques that are in line with governing organizations and sport rules. Using resources available to evaluate opponents is a competitive advantage in preparing the athlete for competition.

Benchmarks
- Analyze opponent's personnel to organize team for competition.
- Create game plans by observation of opponent play, athlete statistical information, and previous competitive experience.
- Make adjustments in strategies for practice and competition by identifying patterns and styles of play of opponents.
- Develop scouting tools for collecting and organizing information about opponents.

Domain 7—Organization and Administration

The coach is an integral resource in the overall administration of the sport program. The coach provides information regarding the needs of the athlete, serves as a key communicator of program goals and policies, and facilitates compliance with established program policies. Program accountability and public trust depend a great deal on the coach's administrative skills.

The coach will:

Standard 30: Demonstrate efficiency in contest management.

The coach must apply administrative skills in the logistics of contest management. Precontest planning will prevent delays and disruptions during the contest. The coach should work with administrators and officials to clarify roles and responsibilities.

Benchmarks
- Make use of sport organization resources in creating a fair and safe competitive environment.
- Ensure athletes have appropriate transportation.
- Provide adequate locker room supervision.
- Take an active role in fostering positive spectator behavior.
- Implement a plan that prepares the facility for competition.
- Create a positive environment that supports officials.

Standard 31: Be involved in public relation activities for the sport program.

Public relations is the responsibility of the coach. Effective communication skills allow the coach to share the mission and values of the program and enlist support from the community. The coach must take every opportunity to be an advocate for the participants in the program.

Benchmarks
- Organize and conduct effective informational meetings before, during, and after the season.
- Communicate policies and ongoing program activities to athletes, staff, parents/guardians, administrators, and/or the public.
- Prepare athletes to be involved with public relation activities.
- Advocate the value of the sport program through positive communication with the media and others.

Standard 32: Manage human resources for the program.

There are many people who contribute to a program's success. The coach must effectively manage staff members to guide them toward meeting goals and objectives of the sport program. The human resources available to the coach must be utilized in an effective manner in order to properly support the athletes they serve.

Benchmarks
- Use multiple methods to communicate regularly with all participants.
- Conduct appropriate screening, training, and supervision for all assistants, managers, captains, and other program personnel.
- Prepare job descriptions and performance objectives for coaching assistants, managers, team captains, and volunteers.
- Be sure all appropriate registration requirements of staff are kept current.

Standard 33: Manage fiscal resources for the program.

The coach must be attentive to the resources and sources of support for the program. Management of the program budget and accountability for expenditures and revenues of the program is a critical responsibility shared by the coach and administration. While program budgets differ, all care must be taken to responsibly manage resources.

Benchmarks
- Follow procedures in utilizing program funds in a fiscally responsible manner.
- Purchase and distribute items that are related to the operation of the sport program in a prudent and equitable manner.
- Demonstrate an ability to maintain accurate and complete financial records.
- Provide clear guidelines for booster clubs and other sources of external support for the program.
- Participate in appropriate fund-raising activities that are in line with governing body regulations.

Standard 34: Facilitate planning, implementation, and documentation of the emergency action plan.

Procedures must be established and implemented to create a safe atmosphere for participants in a sport program. The coach should have documentation to address all areas of the program in order to properly record events leading to injuries. Standard operating procedures should be in place for all aspects of managing the risks of the program.

Benchmarks
- Establish procedures for identifying and correcting unsafe conditions, including stopping, modifying, or moving activity.
- Design and maintain a written record of an emergency action plan for all venues.
- Familiarize coaching assistants, athletes, and parents/guardians of location and use of safety equipment.
- Teach appropriate sport-specific safety procedures to minimize the risk of injuries.
- Complete necessary forms that document each medical emergency.
- Work for the formation of rules that influence the safe and healthy participation of all athletes.

Standard 35: Manage all information, documents, and records for the program.

The coach needs to have procedural manuals relative to all aspects of the program. A systematic process should be established for all information relative to the sport program. Documents should be accessible throughout the season.

Benchmarks
- Maintain records of regular facility inspections, repairs, and requests for maintenance.
- Organize and maintain appropriate records of all practice plans and trainings in the event of legal challenges.
- Prepare and maintain physical examination records, emergency procedures, and injury report forms.
- Have medical history/information available, including parent contact information during each practice/competition.
- Prepare and maintain administrative forms for parent/guardian meetings, athlete eligibility, program evaluation, facility scheduling, travel, and budgeting.
- Disseminate safety procedures with specific definitions of safe environmental conditions, including procedures for stopping the activity.
- Establish, verify, and maintain waivers and participation agreements.

Standard 36: Fulfill all legal responsibilities and risk management procedures associated with coaching.

It is the responsibility of the coach to be proactive in minimizing risk in sport and informing all participants of inherent risks in specific sport situations. The coach must ensure that all aspects of their program are in accordance with recognized standards of care. Understanding the legal responsibilities associated with coaching individual and team events is essential.

Benchmarks
- Follow established transportation policies of the program.
- Ensure that all athletes have appropriate insurance coverage for participation in the program.
- Establish and demonstrate regular review of a formal risk management plan with administrators and medical providers.
- Recognize that full participation of all athletes may require reasonable accommodations in accordance with the Americans with Disabilities Act, and conforming to Title IX or other legislative actions.
- Communicate to coaching assistants, parent/guardians, and athletes the inherent risks associated with sport. Maintain records of informed consent for athletes.
- Provide appropriate supervision for athletes.

Domain 8—Evaluation

The coach needs to be able to make accurate and timely decisions regarding aspects of the sport program. Planning program goals start with a careful analysis of player ability and program needs. Evaluation becomes a critical part of player and staff recruitment and retention as well as of maintaining program accountability. Systematic evaluation ensures that the sport program runs smoothly and efficiently and that the goals and objectives of the program are the focus for the coach, athlete, and team.

The coach will:

***Standard 37:* Implement effective evaluation techniques for team performance in relation to established goals.**

The coach should understand the need for systematic program evaluation. Effective evaluation activities encourage the advancement of team goals, increase public confidence in program benefits, and allow for appropriate program modification to improve performance.

Benchmarks
- Develop a repertoire of appropriate evaluation techniques to use throughout the season.
- Follow an established sequence for evaluation that involves the identification of objectives, data collection, and analysis of data, as well as recommend change when necessary.
- Evaluate practices relative to established goals on the level of competition, individual progress, use of time, and team and/or individual statistics.
- Use seasonal analysis and summary to plan for the off-season and future.
- Assess team outcomes in relation to overall program mission.
- Identify factors that interfere with program success and use these factors to help make program changes.
- Communicate findings of evaluation to respective stakeholders to enhance program growth and support.

***Standard 38:* Use a variety of strategies to evaluate athlete motivation and individual performance as they relate to season objectives and goals.**

Assessment of athlete progress in practices and competition is an important component of coaching. These assessments are critical for the coach to determine how to best prepare and support athletes for practice and competition.

Benchmarks
- Use multiple authentic assessment techniques in practice and games to measure success.
- Use data to assist the athlete in improving performance in ways that respect and motivate the athlete.
- Monitor how well the team members interact with each other or with the coaching staff to improve team cohesion and effort.
- Incorporate evaluation techniques into daily practice plans that provide feedback regarding athlete attitudes toward instructional techniques and level of athlete self-efficacy.

***Standard 39:* Utilize an effective and objective process for evaluation of athletes in order to assign roles or positions and establish individual goals.**

The coach must assess the athlete's ability to perform specific sport-related roles and skills to support decisions about athlete selection and position assignments. How the coach goes about selecting and communicating personnel issues will influence individual motivation and trust. The goal of the coach should be to give an accurate account of the athlete's ability in a sensitive and constructive manner.

Benchmarks
- Establish objective and relevant criteria for the selection/assignment of athletes in contests and/or on teams.
- Seek athlete input and encourage athlete self-evaluation techniques to measure individual progress and performance.

- Provide athletes with evaluations of personal achievement and discuss the results with each athlete at regular intervals.
- Implement diplomatic ways in which to communicate athlete evaluation results.

Standard 40: Utilize an objective and effective process for evaluation of self and staff.

The coach should assess the effectiveness of personnel that directly affect athlete and team performance. The evaluation should collect direct feedback from all program athletes and identify ways to improve techniques and coaching style. Self-evaluation is a critical source of information for professional growth and development.

Benchmarks
- Collect input from athletes, parents, guardians, coaches, and other stakeholders regarding athlete satisfaction, perception of season goals, and coaching performance.
- Conduct periodic self-reflections on coaching effectiveness.
- Seek feedback from experienced coaches to evaluate practice sessions, discuss observations, and implement needed change at regular intervals.
- Use formal written evaluations to assist in selecting and retaining program personnel.
- Be diplomatic when providing feedback on personnel evaluations or hiring decisions.

The Three Levels of Coaching Education

Coaches at all levels of competitive sport should possess at least the minimum competencies for coaching as outlined in *Quality Coaches, Quality Sports: National Standards for Sport Coaches* (2006) before stepping onto the playing or practice field. To ensure an optimal learning environment and the safety and well-being of the athletes, it is imperative that coaches be fully prepared for their responsibilities as a coach.

The national standards show that successful coaching requires certain knowledge and skills that can only be gained through appropriate professional training. There are 40 standards grouped into eight domains. Benchmarks are provided for each standard as examples of varying degrees of progress (e.g., knowledge, skill) toward fully achieving the standard.

It is recognized that not all coaches work with the same skill or competitive level of athletes and teams. For example, there are novice youth sport teams, all-star youth sport travel teams, high school teams, Division I college/university teams, Division III college/university teams, elite teams, and professional teams. Thus, not all coaches require the same level of knowledge and skill for each standard. Because of the variance in the performance level that is needed by different types of coaches, the necessary knowledge and skills are presented in three performance levels: (1) basic coach, (3) intermediate coach, and (5) master coach.

In the first edition of the standards, there were five levels of coaching education. Since several coaching education programs successfully completed the program accreditation process under the five-level system, the numbering system will continue to use 1, 3, and 5, but there will no longer be evaluations at levels 2 and 4. The five-level system will be phased out for the third edition of the *National Standards for Sport Coaches* in order to properly represent those programs currently accredited under the initial accreditation process.

Level 1 represents minimal standards for a basic coach; level 3 represents minimal standards for an intermediate coach; and level 5 represents minimal standards for a master coach. Although the levels represent increasing coaching expertise, typically the standards and benchmarks for basic and intermediate coaches apply to volunteer youth sport coaches, high school coaches, assistant coaches, and beginning collegiate coaches respectively. Most collegiate coaches and all coaches of elite and professional teams and athletes should meet the standards and benchmarks for master coaches. However, coaching competency is not an indication of the level of the athletes that are being coached. For example, a master coach (Level 5) may be found coaching a novice youth sport team.

Below is an example of how the benchmarks for knowledge and skill differ among Level 1, Level 3, and Level 5 coaches. This example is for *Standard 12: Design programs of training, conditioning, and recovery that properly utilize exercise physiology and biomechanical principles.*

Benchmark	Basic Coach	Intermediate Coach	Master Coach
Present conditioning as a prerequisite for athletes to perform at their best, not as punishment.	All athletes must understand that exercise is required to perform at their best and that conditioning is not a punishment, but rather a part of the process of development.	All athletes must understand that exercise is required to perform at their best and that conditioning is not a punishment, but rather a part of the process of development.	All athletes must understand that exercise is required to perform at their best and that specific conditioning practices will enhance their performance.
Know the components of physical fitness and prescribe appropriate levels of each in relation to age- and sport-specific demands.	General fitness knowledge is required. Coaches should use preparation techniques appropriate for activity.	More specific training techniques should be mastered in order to adequately prepare athletes. Coaches should know what drills will improve and enhance athlete performance.	Higher levels of competition will require additional mastery of sport-specific demands and fitness.
Consider the influence of body composition in planning for appropriate practice and conditioning.	General knowledge of health and fitness are necessary to assess athlete performance and capability.	Coaches should have a more in-depth knowledge of exercise physiology as it applies to conducting trainings. Coaches must take into account each athlete as an individual and recognize that certain athletes may require additional attention during conditioning.	Mastery of exercise physiology components are required to train athletes to reach peak performance potential.
Create sport specific warm-up and cool-down activities that accomplish physical and psychological readiness prior to instruction.	Coaches should differentiate between warm-up, play, and cool down. Coaches should help athletes differentiate between practice and competition.	Coaches should understand and target more specifically activities that will fully develop their athletes and enhance performance.	Coaches should understand and target more specifically activities that will fully develop their athletes. Sport-specific warm-up and cool-down activities should be implemented to enhance performance and decrease injury risk.

Benchmark	Basic Coach	Intermediate Coach	Master Coach
Plan a variety of conditioning programs that demonstrate knowledge of physiological responses to physical activity and athletic performance through all phases of the sport season.	Coaches must be able to provide basic knowledge of the sport in season.	Coaches must be able to provide further information for conditioning and skill improvement plans to athletes in pre- and off-seasons.	Coaches must be able to provide detailed information for conditioning and skill improvement plans to athletes for year-round conditioning.
Utilize sound biomechanical principles in the development of training programs that maximize the structural advantages of each athlete.	Coaches must have an awareness of basic strength training in conditioning and prevention of injury.	Coaches must have a mastery of strength training in conditioning and prevention of injury.	Coaches must have a mastery of appropriate training techniques for individual athletes.
Monitor athletes to allow for adequate recovery time to avoid overtraining and maximize windows of optimal training.	All coaches should be able to monitor athlete progress and should have a basic understanding of overtraining and maximal training times.	Coaches should be able to properly manage conditioning programs.	Coaches should be able to properly manage conditioning programs and identify maximal training and recovery times.
Identify and use time efficient cross-training conditioning activities that maximize development of more than one system at a time.	Coaches should demonstrate awareness of proper time management during conditioning activities, as well as cross-training techniques.	Coaches should demonstrate mastery of proper time management during conditioning activities, as well as a mastery of cross-training techniques.	Coaches should demonstrate mastery of appropriate conditioning techniques that are specific to the athletes and the sport.
Avoid training/conditioning activities that are potentially harmful or contraindicated for athletes.	All coaches should be able to identify contraindicated training techniques and avoid them. Coaches should understand proper conditioning methods.	Coaches should demonstrate mastery in designing appropriate conditioning plans.	Coaches should demonstrate mastery and application in designing appropriate conditioning plans.

Because of the diversity of sports and skill/competitive levels of athletes and teams being coached, the standards and benchmarks address only the most common and essential elements of coaching. It is recognized that coach selection, evaluation, and development programs must fit the requirements of various organizations (e.g., national governing bodies, state high school athletic associations, youth sport organizations). Thus, the national standards and benchmarks can be "personalized" for a sport and/or organization as long as the intent of the standard is maintained. For example, in order to adequately address the specialized needs of elite level athletes, the administrators responsible for selecting and/or training these coaches should consider the special qualifications that are needed, including sport-specific knowledge, skill, and experience. Therefore, the emphasis of the national standards document is on the basic knowledge and skills required of coaches at each level and the progression of coaches from a basic coach to an intermediate or master coach as desired.

The national standards are designed to enable education and certification programs to use the resources available to them to help coaching candidates fully understand their responsibilities and master aspects of coaching performance commensurate with the level of athlete and competition in which they are involved. Examples of education/certification programs for master, intermediate, and basic level coaches are provided below.

A master-level coaching principles course should encompass a comprehensive understanding of communication skills, management techniques, and supervisory skills, while being sport-specific with tactical information. All introductory material that is presented at the beginning and intermediate-level courses should be prerequisite information prior to enrolling in and completing the master-level coaching principles course. This course would require maximum contact and instruction time.

An intermediate-level, multi-sport organization coaching principles course should outline overall program philosophies, available resources (such as facilities, equipment, human resources), and age- and skill-appropriate activities. The facilitating organization should require a minimal amount of classroom time in order to accomplish and master all components included in the course, which could take the form of workshops, internships, or apprenticeships (with a minimum number of contact hours required to meet the course requirements) and allow for application of skills and information by the coach candidates.

A basic-level, single-sport coaching principles course should be more of a true introduction to coaching and teaching, rather than cover in-depth, comprehensive information. This course should include teaching tips and learning cues, as well as tips on how to construct practices that allow for maximum exposure to play by the athletes. Typically, basic-level coaches will be volunteers, so shorter workshop and contact time is adequate to be sure that all candidates are exposed to the course and trained before beginning to coach.

It is the responsibility of the coaching education provider to ensure quality preparation of coaching candidates. While any degree of coaching education is good, the higher the quality of the education, the better the environment for the athletes. It is the responsibility of the hiring organization to ensure that their coaches have proper certification that is appropriate for the level of athlete and team that they will be coaching.

By using these standards, NASPE feels strongly that coaching education providers have a strong framework with which to build a quality coaching education program and that coaching candidates who complete such a program will be well-prepared to face the challenges that the coaching profession requires.

Topical Reference

Domain 1—Philosophy and Ethics

Standard 1: Athlete-centered philosophy
- Reasons for entering profession
- Program mission and goals
- Communicate philosophy
- Welcoming behaviors
- Manage athlete behavior

Standard 2: Teach positive values of sport
- Community input
- Diverse population
- Team policies
- Winning
- Lifetime fitness
- Problem solving
- Participation enjoyment

Standard 3: Teach responsible behavior
- Rule application
- Officials
- Respect for others
- Effort and self-control
- Bullying and/or hazing

Standard 4: Demonstrate ethical conduct
- Model good sport behavior
- Exhibit self-control
- Positive language
- Professional relationship
- Personal and official power
- Gambling

Domain 2—Safety and Injury Prevention

Standard 5: Safe facilities
- Facility specifications
- Inspection
- Modify play

Standard 6: Protective equipment
- Safety standards
- Fitting and maintenance
- Selection and use

Standard 7: Environmental conditions
- Environmental safety information
- Facilitate hydration
- Modify play

Standard 8: Physical conditions predisposing injury
- Clearance to participate
- Health status and body structure
- Sleep and emotional states

Standard 9: Immediate care of injuries
- Medical information
- Action plan first aid CPR
- First aid kit
- Communication
- Blood borne pathogens
- Professional medical care
- Injury recovery

Standard 10: Coordinated health care program
- Communication
- Certified trainer
- Decision about returning to play
- Modify coaching techniques

Standard 11: Psychological implications of injury
- Psychological conditions
- Supportive environment
- Anxiety fear of reinjury
- Build self-confidence
- Adherence to rehabilitation
- Poor psychological adjustment

Domain 3—Physical Conditioning

Standard 12: Conditioning based on exercise physiology and biomechanics
- Positive view of conditioning
- Components of physical fitness
- Body composition
- Warm-up and cool-down activities
- Variety of training throughout season
- Biomechanical principles
- Overtraining—periodization
- Cross-training
- Contraindicated activities

Standard 13: Teach proper nutrition
- Timing and selection of food
- Proper hydration options
- Nutrition knowledge
- Body composition weight management
- Eating disorders

Standard 14: Advocate for drug-free sports
- Supplements
- Medications
- Drug use
- Negative consequences drug use
- Social pressure

Standard 15: Conditioning to return to play after injury
- Written permission
- Communication
- Time

Domain 4—Growth and Development

Standard 16: Developmental changes in learning skills
- Sequential developmental training
- Instructional readiness
- Analyze performance
- Maturation levels

Standard 17: Social and emotional growth of athletes
- Age-related social-emotional issues
- Balanced lifestyle
- Lifelong physical activity
- Manage stressors
- Recognize limits

Standard 18: Leadership opportunities
- Personal responsibility
- Athlete input and self-evaluation
- Physical and mental readiness
- Leadership skills
- Manage conflict
- Mentoring opportunities

Domain 5—Teaching and Communication

Standard 19: Positive learning environment
- Individualized instruction
- Team cohesion
- Mistakes
- Corrective instruction
- Behavior management and discipline
- Equal opportunity

Standard 20: Establish goals
- Practice and competition
- Goal-setting process
- Goal difficulty
- Modification of goals
- Mastery goal orientation

Standard 21: Season plan—periodization
- Scope
- Seasonal and sequential planning
- Time
- Communication

Standard 22: Practice management
- Staffing and supervision
- Organize equipment and space
- Waiting time
- Communication
- Diagrams
- Grouping of athletes

Standard 23: Clear instruction
- Teaching progressions
- Learning styles
- Variety instructional methods
- Order and timing of practice activities
- Peer demonstration
- Technology
- Motivation in reteaching

Standard 24: Mental skill training
- Intrinsic and extrinsic rewards
- Stress management
- Build confidence
- Mental game plan
- Improve concentration

Standard 25: Communication
- Terminology
- Expectations
- Orderly environment
- Feedback
- Appropriate language
- Verbal and visual cues
- Overcommunicating

Standard 26: Motivational techniques
- Motivational strategies
- Individual needs
- Burnout
- Achievement environment
- Feedback on success
- Negative discipline
- Self-efficacy

Domain 6—Sport Skills and Tactics

Standard 27: Skills of the sport
- Demonstration of skills
- Performance feedback
- Safety
- Seasonal adjustments

Standard 28: Competitive tactics strategies
- Rules and philosophy
- Situation specific strategies
- Athlete involvement
- Assign positions, line ups
- Game adjustments

Standard 29: Scouting opponents
- Organize team
- Game plan
- Practice planning
- Scouting tools

Domain 7—Organization and Administration

Standard 30: Contest management
- Organization resources
- Transportation
- Locker room supervision
- Spectator behavior
- Facility preparation
- Officials

Standard 31: Public relations
- Informational meetings
- Team policies
- Athlete preparation
- Program advocacy

Standard 32: Manage human resources
- Communication methods
- Training and/or screening of staff
- Job descriptions
- Registration requirements

Standard 33: Manage fiscal resources
- Fiscal responsibility
- Purchasing and distribution
- Financial records
- Guidelines for booster clubs
- Fund-raising

Standard 34: Emergency action plans
- Unsafe conditions
- Written record emergency action plan
- Use of safety equipment
- Sport-specific safety techniques
- Documentation
- Formation of rules

Standard 35: Manage information documents
- Facility
- Practice plans training records
- Physical examination, injury
- Medical history
- Administrative forms
- Eligibility
- Safety procedures
- Waivers and participation agreements

Standard 36: Legal responsibilities
- Transportation
- Insurance
- Risk management plan
- Legislative mandates
- Inherent risks
- Adequate supervision

Domain 8—Evaluation

Standard 37: Team evaluation
- Evaluation tools
- Sequence of evaluation
- Statistics
- Practice evaluation
- Seasonal analysis
- Team outcomes
- Barriers to success
- Communicate findings

Standard 38: Motivation and performance evaluation
- Authentic assessment techniques
- Individual improvement
- Team interactions
- Feedback on instructional techniques

Standard 39: Player selection
- Criteria for selection
- Competition data
- Athlete input—self evaluation
- Feedback to athletes
- Communicate evaluation

Standard 40: Staff and self-evaluation
- External input
- Self-reflection
- Peer-feedback
- Formal evaluations
- Diplomacy

Programs

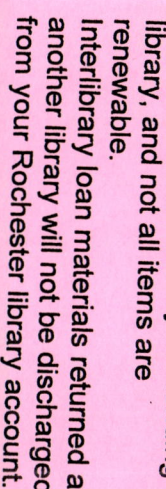

...ity training of coaches. These resources include
...referenced within a comprehensive coaching
...ecome available and current information should

and analysis for teachers. *Journal of Physical Education, Recreation & Dance, 67*(8), 20-23.

American College of Sports Medicine. (2005a). *ACSM's guidelines for exercise testing and prescription* (7th ed.). Philadelphia: Lippincott Williams & Wilkins.

American College of Sports Medicine. (2005b). *ACSM's resource manual for guidelines for exercise testing and prescription* (5th ed.). Philadelphia: Lippincott Williams & Wilkins.

American Football Coaches Association. (1995). *Football coaching strategies*. Champaign, IL: Human Kinetics.

Ammon, R., Jr., Southall, R. M., & Blair, D. A. (2004). *Sport facility management: Organizing events and mitigating risks*. Morgantown, WV: Fitness Information Technology.

Ammons, D. N. (2001). *Municipal benchmarks: Assessing local performance and established community standards* (2nd ed.). Thousand Oaks, CA: Sage.

Anders, E., & Myers, S. (1999). *Field hockey: Steps to success*. Champaign, IL: Human Kinetics.

Anderson, J. C., Courson, R. W., Kleinger, D. M., & McLoda, T. A. (2002). National Athletic Trainers' Association position statement: Emergency planning in athletics. *Journal of Athletic Training, 37*(1), 99-104.

Anshel, M. (1997). *Sport psychology: From theory to practice*. Scottsdale, AZ: Gorsuch Scarisbrick.

Appenzeller, H. (2005). *Risk management in sport: Issues and strategies* (2nd ed.). Durham, NC: Carolina Academic.

Aston, G. (2003, August 6). E&M guidelines, emergency care rules under HHS review. *American Medical News*, pp. 5.

Baechle, T., & Earle, R. (2001). *Essentials of strength training and conditioning* (2nd ed.). Champaign, IL: Human Kinetics.

Barth, M. M., Hatem, J. J., & Yang, B. Z. (2004). A pedagogical note on risk framing. *Risk Management and Insurance Review, 7*(2), 151.

Bennis, W. (1989). *On becoming a leader*. Reading, MA: Addison-Wesley.2

Berg, K. E., & Latin, R. W. (2003). *Essentials of research methods in health, physical education, exercise science, and recreation* (2nd ed.). Philadelphia: Lippincott Williams & Wilkins.

Biddle, S. (Ed.). (1995). *European perspectives on exercise and sport psychology.* Champaign, IL: Human Kinetics.

Blanchard, K. (1995). *The anthropology of sport: An introduction* (Revised ed.). Westport, CT: Bergin & Garvey.

Blanksby, B. A., Bloomfield, J., Ackland, T. R., Elliott, B. C., & Morton, A. R. (1994). *Athletics, growth and development in children.* Langhorne, PA: Harwood Academic.

Bowers, A. W., & Fox, E. L. (1992). *Sport physiology.* Dubuque, IA: W. C. Brown.

Bowker, L. H. (1998). *Masculinities and violence.* Thousand Oaks, CA: Sage.

Bridges, D. M. (1999). *Cultural bias in sport and play.* Reston, VA: American Association for Active Lifestyles and Fitness.

Brooks, D., & Althouse, R. (2000). *Racism in college athletics: The African-American athlete's experience.* Morgantown, WV: Fitness Information Technology.

Byra, M. (1992). Measuring qualitative aspects of teaching in physical education. *Journal of Physical Education, Recreation & Dance, 63*(3), 83.

Carr, G. (1996). *Mechanics of sport: A practitioner's guide.* Champaign, IL: Human Kinetics.

Chamberlin, C., & Lee, T. (1993). *Arranging practice conditions and designing instruction.* In R. N. Singer, M. Murphey, and K. L. Tenant (Eds.), *Handbook of research on sport psychology* (pp. 213-241). New York: MacMillan.

Chu, D. (1992). *Jumping into plyometrics.* Champaign, IL: Leisure.

Clifford, C. E. (1997). *Coaching for character: Reclaiming the principles of sportsmanship.* Champaign, IL: Human Kinetics.

Coakley, J. (2004) *Sport and society: Issues and controversies* (8th ed.). New York: McGraw-Hill.

Colson, J. L. (2002). *Emergency medical services sourcebook: Basic consumer health information about preventing, preparing for and managing emergency situations.* Detroit: Omnigraphics.

Costa, D., & Guthrie, S. (1994). *Women in sport: Interdisciplinary perspectives.* Champaign, IL: Human Kinetics.

Cox, R. (1994). *Sport psychology: Concepts and applications* (3rd ed.). Dubuque, IA: Brown and Benchmark.

Cratty, B. (1989). *Psychology in contemporary sport* (3rd ed.). Englewood Cliffs, NJ: Prentice-Hall.

Creedon, P. J. (1994). *Women, media and sport: Challenging gender values.* Thousand Oaks, CA: Sage.

Davis, R. (2002). *Inclusion through sports: A guide to enhancing sport experiences.* Champaign, IL: Human Kinetics.

DeRenne, C., & House, T. (1993). *Power baseball.* St. Paul, MN: West.

Donnelly, J. E. (1990). *Living anatomy.* Champaign, IL: Leisure.

Drucker, P. (1992). *Managing for the future.* New York: Penguin Books USA.

Duda, J. L. (1998). *Advances in sport and exercise psychology measurement.* Morgantown, WV: Fitness Information Technology.

Dutta, A., & Proctor, R. W. (1995). *Skill acquisition and human performance.* Thousand Oaks, CA: Sage.

Eitzen, D. (1982). *Sociology of American sport.* Dubuque, IA: W. C. Brown.

Eitzen, D. (1993). *Sport in contemporary society: An anthology.* New York: St. Martin's.

Emergency Nurses Association. (2000). *Emergency nursing core curriculum* (5th ed.). Philadelphia: W. B. Saunders.

Evans, T. (Ed.). (1986). *Physical education, sport and schooling: Studies in the sociology of physical education.* Philadelphia: Falmer.

Figler, S. (1981). *Sport and play in American life: A textbook in the sociology of sport.* Philadelpha: Saunders College.

Figler, S. (1995). *Sport.* Dubuque, IA: Brown & Benchmark.

Flegel, M. J. (2004). *Sports first aid* (3rd ed.). Champaign, IL: Human Kinetics.

Ford, C. W. (1994). *We CAN all get along: 50 steps you can take to help end racism.* New York: Dell.

Fry, R., Morton, A., & Keast, D. (1991). Overtraining in athletes: An update. *Sports Medicine, 12*(1), 32-65.

Funk, G. D. (1991). *Major violation: The unbalanced priorities in athletics and academics.* Champaign, IL: Human Kinetics.

Gallagher, E. J., Lombardi, G., & Gennis, P. (1995). Effectiveness of bystander cardiopulmonary resuscitation and survival following out-of-hospital cardiac arrest. *Journal of the American Medical Association, 274*(24), 1922-1925.

Gill, D. (1986). *Psychological dynamics of sport.* Champaign, IL: Human Kinetics.

Glisan, E. M. (2003). *Life skills academics: Health: Making healthy choices in everyday life.* Verona, WI: IEP Resources.

Gordon, R. (1993). *The social psychology of sport.* New York: Springer-Verlag.

Gould, D. (2000). *Tennis, anyone?* Mt. View, CA: Mayfield.

Granatt, M. (2004). On trust: Using public information and warning partnerships to support the community response to an emergency. *Journal of Communication Management, 8*(4), 354-365.

Gustafson, J. (1986). Observing two important teaching variables to evaluate teaching. *Physical Educator, 43*(3), 146.

Haff, G., & Potteiger, J. A. (1997). Creatine supplementation for the strength/power athlete. *Strength and Conditioning Journal, 19*(6), 72-74.

Hall, S. J. (2002). *Basic biomechanics* (4th ed.). New York: McGraw-Hill.

Harris, J. C. (1994). *Athletes and the American hero dilemma.* Champaign, IL: Human Kinetics.

Henschen, K. P. (1995). *Sport psychology: An analysis of athlete behavior* (3rd ed.). Ithaca, NY: Mouvement.

Heyward, V. H. (2002). *Advanced fitness assessment and exercise prescription* (4th ed.). Champaign, IL: Human Kinetics.

Hoeger, W. K., & Hoeger, S. A. (2002). *Principles and labs for fitness and wellness* (8th ed.). Belmont, CA: Brooks Cole.

Horn, T. S. (Ed.). (1992). *Advances in sport psychology.* Champaign, IL: Human Kinetics.

Houston, M. E. (2001). *Biochemistry primer for exercise science.* Champaign, IL: Human Kinetics.

Howard, E., & Wiseman, K. (2001). Emergency and disaster planning: Patient education and preparation. *Nephrology Nursing Journal, 28*(5), 527.

Hyde, C. L. (2002). *Fitness instructor training guide.* Dubuque, IA: Kendall/Hunt.

Insel, P. M., & Roth, W. T. (2004). *Core concepts in health* (9th ed.). New York: McGraw-Hill.

Jackson, S., & Marsh, H. (1986). Athletic or antisocial? The female sport experience. *Journal of Sport Psychology, 8,* 198-211.

Janssen, J. (2002). *Championship team building: What every coach needs to know to build a motivated, committed and cohesive team.* Tucson, AZ: Winning the Mental Game.

Janssen, J., & Dale, G. (2001). *The seven secrets of successful coaches: How to unlock and unleash your team's full potential.* Cary, NC: Janssen Peak Performance.

Johnson, R. E., & LaVoy, B. (1989). Fitness testing for children with special needs: An alternative approach. *Journal of Physical Education, Recreation & Dance, 60*(6), 50-53.

Jones, S. A., Joy, M. P., & Pearson, J. (2002). Forecasting demand of emergency care. *Health Care Management Science, 5*(4), 297.

Karlsson, J. (1997). *Antioxidants and exercise.* Champaign, IL: Human Kinetics.

Kaszynski, S. B. (2001). EMTALA: Duty extends to even non-transferring emergency patients. *The Journal of Law, Medicine & Ethics, 29*(1), 102.

King, H. A., & Aufsesser, K. S. (1988). Criterion-referenced testing: An ongoing process. *Journal of Physical Education, Recreation & Dance, 59*(1), 58-63.

Knox, K. L., Conwell, Y., & Caine, E. D. (2004). If suicide is a health problem, what are we doing to prevent it? *American Journal of Public Health, 94*(1), 37-45.

Knudson, D. V., & Morrison, C. S. (1997). *Qualitative analysis of human movement.* Champaign, IL: Human Kinetics.

Kraemer, W. J., Fleck, S. J., & Deschenes, M. (1988). Factors in exercise prescription of resistance training. *National Strength & Conditioning Association Journal, 10*(5), 36-42.

Lapchick, R. E. (Ed.). (1996). *Sport in society: Equal opportunity or business as usual?* Thousand Oaks, CA: Sage.

Laughlin, N., & Laughlin, S. (1992). The myth of measurement in physical education. *Journal of Physical Education, Recreation & Dance, 63*(4), 83-85.

Launder, A. G. (2001). *Play practice: The games approach to teaching and coaching sports.* Champaign, IL: Human Kinetics.

LeUnes, A., & Nation, J. R. (2001). *Sport psychology* (3rd ed.). Belmont, CA: Wadsworth.

Levy, B. S., & Sidel, V. W. (2002). *Terrorism and public health: A balanced approach to strengthening systems and protecting people.* Oxford: Oxford University.

Locke, E. A., Latham, G. P., Smith, K. J., & Wood, R. E. (1990). *A theory of goal setting and task performance.* Englewood Cliffs, NJ: Prentice-Hall.

Lumpkin, A., Stoll, S. K., & Beller, J. M. (2002). *Sport ethics: Applications for fair play* (3rd ed.). New York: McGraw-Hill.

Luttgans, K., & Hamilton, N. (2001). *Kinesiology: Scientific basis of human motion* (10th ed.). New York: McGraw-Hill.

Maglischo, E. W. (1993). *Swimming even faster.* Mountain View, CA: Mayfield.

Martens, R. (2004). *Successful coaching: America's best selling coach's guide* (3rd ed.). Champaign, IL: Human Kinetics.

McArdle, W. D., Katch, F. I., & Katch, V. L. (2004). *Exercise physiology: Energy, nutrition, and human performance* (5th ed.). Philadelphia: Lippincott Williams & Wilkins.

McArdle, W. D., Katch, F. I., & Katch, V. L. (2005). *Sports & exercise nutrition* (2nd ed.). Philadelphia: Lippincott Williams & Wilkins.

Melnyk, B. M., & Fineout-Overholt, E. (2004). *Evidence-based practice in nursing & healthcare: A guide to best practice.* Philadelphia: Lippincott Williams & Wilkins.

Millman, D. (1994). *The inner athlete: Realizing your fullest potential.* Walpole, NH: Stillpoint.

Nakamura, R. M. (1996) *The power of positive coaching.* Boston: Jones & Bartlett.

Nanus, B. (1991). *The seven keys to leadership in a turbulent world.* New York: McGraw-Hill.

Nicholl, J., & Munro, J. (2000). Systems for emergency care. *British Medical Journal, 320*(7240), 955-956.

NOW Legal Defense and Education Fund. (1999). *Sexual harassment in the schools: Legal resource kit.* New York: Author.

Paludi, M. A. (1991). *Ivory power: Sexual harassment on campus.* Albany, NY: State University of New York.

Penick, H., & Shrake, B. (1999). *Harvey Penick's little red book: Lessons and teachings from a lifetime in golf.* New York: Simon & Schuster.

Phillips, A., & Carlisle, C. (1983). The physical education teacher assessment instrument. *Journal of Teaching in Physical Education, 2*(2), 62.

Plagenhoef, S. (1971). *Patterns of human motion: A cinematographic analysis.* Englewood Cliffs, NJ: Prentice-Hall.

Plisk, S. S., & Kreider, R. B. (1999). Creating controversy? *Strength and Conditioning Journal, 21*(1), 14-23.

Potteiger, J. A., & Wilson, G. D. (1989a). Training the pitcher: A hypothetical model. *National Strength & Conditioning Association Journal, 11*(3), 27-31.

Potteiger, J. A., & Wilson, G. D. (1989b). Training the pitcher: A physiological perspective. *National Strength & Conditioning Association Journal, 11*(3), 24-26.

Reade, B. (1993). *Coaching football successfully.* Champaign, IL: Human Kinetics.

Reynolds, M. C. (Ed.). (1989). *Knowledge base for the beginning teachers.* Oxford: Pergamon.

Robergs, R. A., & Roberts, S. O. (1997). *Exercise physiology: Exercise, performance, and clinical applications.* Dubuque, IA: William C. Brown.

Robertson, M. A. (1984). *Developing children: Their changing movement.* Philadelphia: Lea & Febiger.

Rosenboom, K. (1992). The Wichita state program. *National Strength & Conditioning Association Journal, 14*(1), 10-13.

Rotella, B., Boyce, B. A., Allyson, B., & Savis, J. C. (Eds.). (1997). *Case studies in sport psychology.* Boston: Jones & Bartlett.

Rowe, C. A. (2004). Managing risk in the public sector. *Risk Management Magazine, 51*(11), 52.

Sargent, R. G., & Hohn, E. (1988). Protein needs for the athlete. *National Strength & Conditioning Association Journal, 10*(4), 53-55.

Sherwood, L. (2005). *Fundamentals of physiology: A human perspective* (3rd ed.). Belmont, CA: Brooks Cole.

Shields, D. L. L., & Bredemeier, B. J. L. (1995). *Character development and physical activity.* Champaign, IL: Human Kinetics.

Siedentop, D., & Tannehill, D. (1999). *Developing teaching skills in physical education* (4th ed.). Mountain View, CA: Mayfield.

Sharkey, B. J. (1986). *Coaches guide to sport physiology.* Champaign, IL: Human Kinetics.

Silverstein, A., Silverstein, V., & Nunn, L. S. (2000). *Staying safe.* New York: Franklin Watts.

Singer, R. N. (1984). *Sustaining motivation in sport.* Tallahassee, FL: Sport Consultants International.

Smith, N., & Messina, L. M. (Eds.). (2004). *Homeland security.* Bronx, NY: H. W. Wilson.

Sorum, P. C. (1995). Deciding about cardiopulmonary resuscitation: The contributions of decision making. *Archives of Internal Medicine, 155*(5), 513-521.

Spengler, J. O. (2002). Automated external defibrillators in sport, physical education and recreation settings: Emerging litigation. *Journal of Physical Education, Recreation & Dance, 73*(2), 6-7.

Starr, C., & McMillan, B. (1999). *Human biology* (6th ed.). Belmont, CA: Brooks Cole.

Stone, M., & O'Bryant, H. S. (1986). *Weight training: A scientific approach.* Minneapolis, MN: Burgess International Group.

Thomasen, E., & Rist, R. A. (1996). *Anatomy and kinesiology for ballet teachers.* Hightstown, NJ: Princeton Book.

Trimble, A. (2005). *Coaching football successfully.* Champaign, IL: Human Kinetics.

Van Raalte, J. L., & Brewer, B. W. (Eds.) (2002). *Exploring sport and exercise psychology* (2nd ed.). Washington, DC: American Psychological Association.

Vincent, W. J. (2005). *Statistics in kinesiology* (3rd ed.). Champaign, IL: Human Kinetics.

Von Elm, E. (2004). Prehospital emergency care and the global road safety crisis. *Journal of the American Medical Association, 292*(8), 923.

Wade, J. (2004). Reducing the threat. *Risk Management Magazine, 51*(11), 10.

Wang, J., & Wiese-Bjornstal, D. M. (1994). Mechanical and anatomical analysis of the soccer instep shot. *Strength and Conditioning, 16*(6), 34-38.

Wathen, D. (1993). Literature review: Explosive/plyometric exercises. *National Strength & Conditioning Association Journal, 15*(3), 17-19.

Wathen, D. (2003). Website of the week: Bioterrorism. *British Medical Journal, 326*(7382), 230.

Weinberg, R. S., & Gould, D. (2003). *Foundations of sport and exercise psychology* (3rd ed.). Champaign, IL: Human Kinetics.

Welheiser, J., & Scott, J. (2002). *An ounce of preparation: Integrated disaster planning for archives, libraries and record centers* (2nd ed.). Lanham, MD: Scarecrow.

Wiggins, D. K. (1997). *Glory bound: Black athletes in a white America.* Syracuse, NY: Syracuse University.

Williams, J. M. (Ed.). (2005). *Applied sport psychology: Personal growth to peak performance* (5th ed.). New York: McGraw-Hill.

Wilmore, J. H., & Costill, D. L. (2004). *Physiology of sport and exercise* (3rd ed.). Champaign, IL: Human Kinetics.

United States Tennis Association. (2004). *Coaching tennis successfully* (2nd ed.). Champaign, IL: Human Kinetics.

Yesalis, C. E. (Ed.). (2000). *Anabolic steroids in sport and exercise* (2nd ed.). Champaign, IL: Human Kinetics.

Glossary

Affective skills: The ability to understand and to deal effectively with emotions, feelings, and moods.

Americans with Disabilities Act: The law requiring programs to make reasonable accommodations that facilitate full and equal enjoyment of an activity by qualified individuals with a disability. For more information, please visit www.ADA.gov.

Assessment: The process of gathering evidence that provides information for use in monitoring performance, making decisions, and improving programs.

Authentic assessment: The process of evaluating learning as demonstrated through performance of a skill or knowledge in a real-life setting.

Benchmark: A description or example of performance that serves as evidence for evaluation or judgment.

Best practices: Activities or styles that have been deemed appropriate by the profession and result in positive outcomes.

Causal attributions: The perception of causality, stability, and controllability of the sources of success or failure.

Cognitive readiness: Having the mental prerequisites necessary for processing information, creating a motor plan, and evaluating various types of feedback in order to execute a skill.

Contraindicated: Practices that increase the risk of injury and are potentially harmful or inadvisable, such as certain training, conditioning, and teaching activities.

Disordered eating patterns: Eating habits that are not conducive to good health. These can take many forms, including binging, purging, undereating, overeating, and switching back and forth between habits.

Emergency action plan: An established protocol for handling of injuries or situations at specific venues, including management of individual injury and notification of emergency personnel.

Evaluation: A comparison measuring performance with established standards.

Extrinsic rewards: A form of performance feedback originating from an external source rather than from the activity's inherent enjoyment or personal satisfaction.

Fiscal responsibility: Using program resources in accord with established policies and regulations.

Games-based teaching technique: Using the context of competition to introduce or refine skills. This requires modification or regulation of game play to accomplish specific learning objectives.

Goal-setting process: A series of steps that identify measurable standards of desired behavior or behavior change and the resources and actions necessary to achieve that standard.

Hazing: Any action or event conducted with the purpose of ridiculing or humiliating individuals for the intent of group initiation, and which may be harmful and/or illegal.

Intrinsic rewards: Perceptions of competence, control, or enjoyment from performing an activity.

Learning styles: The way individuals take in and retain new information in developing skills.

Low-risk training practices: Conditioning activities that provide an appropriate level of overload while minimizing potential for physical injury.

Mastery goal orientation: To view perceptions of ability or accomplishment as a function of effort and improvement.

Mental skills: Learned systematic regulation of cognitive processes to enhance performance, increase enjoyment, and/or achieve self-satisfaction.

Overcoaching: To provide an excessive amount of instructional information, feedback, and/or controlling behaviors, thus causing performance decrement and lower athlete satisfaction.

Overtraining: Too much training overload or too little training recovery that results in diminished physical adaptations, possible injury, or psychological burnout.

Pedagogy: General concepts, theories, and research about effective teaching.

Performance-based goals (versus outcome): An established standard of behavior relatively independent of others' performance; therefore, there is no interpersonal comparison.

Performance indicators: Evidence of behaviors that reflect understanding of knowledge and mastery of skills in a specific coaching domain or standard.

Periodization: Division of the yearly training plan into smaller, easier to manage training phases with loads that increase progressively and cyclically to optimize performance. Training is designed to allow for overload and adaptation by the inclusion of recovery techniques throughout the program.

Exercise physiology: The study of the processes and functions of the human body as influenced by the performance of any physical activity.

Positive discipline strategies: Plans to reduce unwanted behaviors by reinforcing desired behaviors, communicating clear behavioral expectations, and providing encouragement.

Scouting: Methods of evaluating upcoming opponents to better prepare athletes for competition. Some techniques that can be used include observation, video, and statistical review. In terms of youth sports, this could be as simple as evaluating whether or not the opposing team has enough players to field a team for a game.

Self-determination: A person's motivation to demonstrate competence, connect to others when performing a task, and feel a sense of personal initiative or control.

Self-efficacy: Athletes' judgment of their capabilities for a specific learning outcome or performing a specific task.

Self-reflection: To consider if one's actions have brought about intended outcomes, or if there are improvements to be made.

Sexual harassment: Unwanted behaviors, gestures, or comments that either directly ask for sexual favors or create a hostile environment or uncomfortable situation that interferes with the full participation of an individual.

Stakeholders: Those involved in a sport program, including athletes, parents, guardians, coaches, and other staff members who contribute to the operation of the organization.

Standards: Written expectations for what coaches should be able to know and do.

Strategy: Competitive decisions made by an individual or a team about overall play of the game.

Systematic instructional techniques: A planned sequence of teaching strategies that promotes learning through progression of skills.

Tactics: An individual or teams actions about when, why, and how to respond to a particular game situation.

Team cohesion: The degree to which members of a team get along with each other and are committed to work together to achieve a specific and identifiable goal.

Time-on-task: The amount of active or meaningful engagement in a learning activity.

Title IX: The law enacted to relieve the disparity of education-based sport programs. The law requires institutions to provide equal educational opportunities for boys and girls. For more information, please visit www.titleix.info.

Whole-part teaching technique: Instructional strategies that provide opportunity to practice the entire skill, followed by activities that emphasize part of the skill.

Windows of trainability: Optimal times in the physical maturation of athletes to improve performance, including increasing speed, strength, and other physical attributes.

NASPE Resources

Published by the National Association for Sport and Physical Education for quality sport and physical education programs:

Coaching Documents

Quality Coaches, Quality Sports: National Standards for Sport Coaches, 2nd Edition (2006), Stock No. 304-10274

Developing Strength in Children and Adolescents: A Comprehensive Guide, 2nd Edition (2007), Stock No. 304-10292

Coaching Issues & Dilemmas: Character Dilemma: Character Building through Sport Participation (2003), Stock No. 304-10270

Coaching Education: Designing Quality Programs (2001), Stock No. 304-10243

Physical Activity & Sport for Secondary School Students. 5th Edition (2002), Stock No. 304-10250

Principles of Safety in Sport & Physical Education, 3rd Edition (2002), Stock No. 304-10251

Liability & Safety in Physical Education & Sport (2002), Stock No. 304-10252

Coaching Position Papers

Program Orientation for High School Sport Coaches (2005)

Coaching the Parents (2003)

Rights and Responsibilities of Interscholastic Athletes (2003)

Co-Curricular Physical Activity and Sport Programs for Middle School Students (2002)

Guidelines for After-School Physical Activity and Intramural Sport Programs (2002)

Coaches Code of Conduct (2001)

Sexual Harassment in Athletic Settings (2000)

Choosing the Right Sport and Physical Activity Program for Your Child (1999)

Physical Education Documents

Moving into the Future: National Standards for Physical Education, 2nd Edition (2004), Stock No. 304-10275

National Standards for Beginning Physical Education Teachers, 2nd Edition (2003)

Physical Activity for Children: A Statement of Guidelines for Children Ages 5-12, 2nd Edition (2003), Stock No. 304-10276

Active Start: A Statement of Physical Activity Guidelines for Children Birth to Five Years (2002), Stock No. 304-10254

Movement-Based Learning: Academic Concepts and Physical Activity for Ages Three through Eight (2006), 304-10300

Physical Educators' Guide to Successful Grant Writing (2005), 304-10291

On Your Mark, Get Set, Go!: A Guide for Beginning Physical Education Teachers (2004), 304-10264

National Physical Education Standards in Action (2003), 304-10267

Teaching Games for Understanding in Physical Education & Sport (2003), Stock No. 304-10266

Beyond Activities: Elementary Volume (2003), Stock No. 304-10265

Beyond Activities: Secondary Volume (2003), Stock No. 304-10268

Concepts and Principles of Physical Education: What Every Student Needs to Know (2003), Stock No. 304-10261

Appropriate Practice Documents

Appropriate Practice in Movement Programs for Young Children, Ages 3-5 (2000), Stock No. 304-10232

Appropriate Practice ... *Education* (2000), Stock No. 304-10230

Appropriate Practices for M... ..., Stock No. 304-10248

Appropriate Practices for High School Physical Education (2004), Stock No. 304-10272

Opportunity to Learn Documents

Opportunity to Learn Standards for Elementary Physical Education (2000), Stock No. 304-10242

Opportunity to Learn Standards for Middle School Physical Education (2004), Stock No. 304-10290

Opportunity to Learn Standards for High School Physical Education (2004), Stock No. 304-10289

Assessment Series

Assessing Gymnastics in Elementary Physical Education (2006), Stock No. 304-10303

Assessing Dance in Elementary Physical Education (2005), Stock No. 304-10304

Assessment of Swimming in Physical Education (2005), Stock No. 304-10301

Assessing Concepts: Secondary Biomechanics (2004), Stock No. 304-10220

Assessing Student Outcomes in Sport Education (2003), Stock No. 304-10219

Assessment in Outdoor Adventure Physical Education (2003), Stock No. 304-10218

Assessing Heart Rate in Physical Education (2002), Stock No. 304-10214

Authentic Assessment of Physical Activity for High School Students (2002), Stock No. 304-10216

Elementary Heart Health: Lessons and Assessment (2001), Stock No. 304-10215

Portfolio Assessment for K-12 Physical Education (2000), Stock No. 304-10213

Assessing Motor Skills in Elementary Physical Education (1999), Stock No. 304-10207

Assessment in Games Teaching (1999), Stock No. 304-10212

Creating Rubrics for Physical Education (1999), Stock No. 304-10209

Order online at www.naspeinfo.org or call 1-800-321-0789

Shipping and handling additional.

National Association for Sport and Physical Education,
an association of the American Alliance for Health, Physical Education, Recreation, and Dance

1900 Association Drive, Reston, VA 20191, naspe@aahperd.org, 703-476-3410